PIGEON TO PACKHORSE

The Illustrated Story of Animals in Army Communications

By Alan Harfield

PICTON PUBLISHING (CHIPPENHAM) LTD
1989

First Published by Picton Publishing (Chippenham) Ltd. 1989
ISBN 0948251 42 5

British Library Cataloguing in Publication Data
Harfield, Alan
Pigeon to Packhorse:
The story of animals in communication
1. Armies   Communication
I. Title
355.27

Printed in Great Britain by Picton Print
Citadel Works, Bath Road, Chippenham, Wilts.

Contents

Acknowledgements —————————————————————— V

Frontispiece ————————————————————————— VII

Chapters

1. The Telegraph Troop ————————————————— 1
2. Animal Transport In India ————————————— 13
3. The Cable Wagon and the Cable Cart ————————— 29
4. Camels and Communications ———————————— 61
5. The Advent of the Wireless ———————————— 65
6. Messenger Dogs ————————————————— 85
7. The Pigeon Service ————————————————— 91
8. Horses for Courses ———————————————— 103

Bibliography ——————————————————————— 109

Index —————————————————————————— 110

Line drawings at pages 12, 35, 51, 80 and 84 are from the Manual of Horsemastership, Equitation and Animal Transport, 1937.

Line Drawings at pages 95 and 102 are from the Manual of Instruction for the use of homing pigeons in India and South East Asia.

Acknowledgements

The information contained in this publication has been obtained from the Archives of the Royal Signals Museum and from the references given in the Bibliography. The majority of the illustrations are also from the Royal Signals Museum photographic collection.

I extend my grateful thanks to Major Roger Pickard, the Curator of the Royal Signals Museum, for his help with the selection of material and advice in respect of the wireless equipment used during the years prior to the mechanisation of the Corps.

August 1988.   AH

V

Position of 'Attention' mounted.

Royal Signals Officer in Full Dress,
circa 1937.

From a Painting by Gilbert Holiday
(Courtesy of the Royal Signals Museum).

VII

Chapter 1
The Telegraph Troop

The change from the use of visual signalling to the electric telegraph during the war in the Crimea in 1854 marks the start of the use of animals as part of the military communication network in the 19th century. Prior to this time, of course, animals were used as messages were passed between Commanders in the field and their brigades and regiments by the use of mounted messenger. These despatches were, in the main, entrusted to young officers who were attached to the staff of the General and who were well-mounted and able riders. The reason for the use of young officers in this capacity was due to the fact that the majority of the men serving in the ranks, during the Peninsular and Waterloo campaigns, were unable to read and write. There were, of course, exceptions as a number of diaries and letters exist in archives, giving graphic descriptions of service in these campaigns. It was accepted that junior officers would perform these duties and, at the outset of the war in the Crimea, this situation still existed. When acting in this capacity the officer rode his own horse so that there was no need for additional training to be given either to horse or the rider.

Events occurred which changed the whole concept of army communications and the first of these was in 1837 when Sir William Cooke and Professor Sir Charles Wheatstone designed and introduced the electric telegraph. At the same time Samuel Morse was perfecting his invention of the Morse Code. With the commencement of the war in the Crimea, in 1854, the Electric Telegraph Company placed its services and stores at the disposal of the Government and the electric telegraph was employed in war for the first time. The overland cable proved to be no problem but it was necessary for a 340-mile submarine cable to be laid from Varna, on the coast of Dobrudscha, under the Black Sea, to Balaclava. In addition to this permanent means of communication between the theatre of war and the Government in the United Kingdom it was necessary to establish a field unit.

It was the formation of this unit that brought the use of animals into the communication network. The new unit was organised within the Royal Sappers and Miners (later to become the Corps of Royal Engineers) and was commanded, initially, by Lieutenant George Montague Stopford. The unit had 25 sappers equipped with two horse-drawn telegraph office wagons, a cable cart and a plough and was also supplied with 24 miles of copper wire which was insulated with thick gutta-percha. Due to the inclement weather it was not possible for the field cable to be laid until late February 1855 and even then the ground was so frozen that the plough made little or no impression on the soil. The men therefore had to dig the trench for the cable. Among the other problems that the unit encountered was the fact that the insulation attracted field mice who through eating the insulation caused breaks in the wire. However by the end of the campaign 21 miles of cable had been laid and eight offices were established on the circuit. The new means of communication was considered to be a success, though Lord Raglan, the

Cavalry Staff Corps,
(Courtesy of W. Y. Carman).

Commander-in-Chief, felt that he was too much under the control of the War Department and commented that ". . . the telegraph has upset everything . . ." The use of horse drawn telegraph offices and cable carts had been established and then became a part of the communication organisation.

Following the end of the Crimean campaign there was a move to form a Signal unit to deal with army communication, and after the technical advances made during the American Civil War it was agreed that a Signal Wing would be formed at the Royal Engineers School at Chatham. A Field Telegraph Train was established and this section provided the 'neutral' signals during the Volunteer Manoeuvres which were held at Dover on Easter Monday 1869. An account of the field training

The Field Telegraph Train at Dover, 1869. The Office Wagon. *(The Illustrated London News)*

The Field Telegraph Train at Dover, 1869. The Cable Wagon. (*The Illustrated London News*).

appeared in the *Illustrated London News* and shows a horse drawn Field Telegraph Office wagon and the horse drawn Cable wagon in use.

In the following year the Government approved the formation of a new unit, within the Corps of Royal Engineers, to deal with army communications. The unit was given the title of C Telegraph Troop, RE and came into being on 1 September 1870 under the command of Captain Montague Lambert. The stated duty of C Troop was to provide telegraph communications for the 'field army' and for this task the establishment of the troops was set as:

". . .5 officers, 245 non-commissioned officers and men and 150 horses. . ."

The actual strength, recorded by Captain Lambert on the formation of the troops, was:-

Officers
Captain 1; Lieutenant 1;

NCOs and Men
Sergeants 7; NCOs & Men 126. Total all ranks — 135.

Horses
Riding 30: Draught 25. Total — 55

The Record of Service of 'C Troop' shows the following details concerning the equipment of the new troop:

". . .The duties to be performed by the Troop consist in the carriage, charge, and working of 36 miles of insulated cable with all the necessary stores supplemented by visual signalling, for which purpose a body of drivers, 20 in number, are equipped as mounted signallers.

The number of carriages are as follows:

Wire	Office	Pontoon	Forge	Store	Total
12	4	1	1	6	24

The wire, office and pontoon wagons are constructed with springs, a novelty in military carriages, and are lighter than those in general use at this date for military purposes. . ."

The main item of transport was the Wire wagon and each wagon carried three miles of cable on six drums, and the boxes on the wire wagons carried all the other necessary stores such as the jointers, pliers etc and, of course, the arms of the detachment allocated to the wagon. The account of C Troop records that the cable was generally laid out along roads and when a road has to be crossed ". . .iron telescopic poles are put up, and the cable is thus raised high enough to allow carriages passing beneath. . ." The office wagon was used to transport the instruments and all writing materials etc for the field telegraph office.

After a proving exercise in May 1871, when the troop successfully laid a line from Brompton Barracks to a signal station that had been set up near Sittingbourne,

C Telegraph Troop on parade at Chatham, 1870.

Cable Wagon, circa 1870. Also referred to as 'The Wire Wagon'.

The Cable, or Wire Wagon, circa 1870.

Pontoon, or Boat Wagon, circa 1870.

Office Wagon, RE, circa 1870.

C (Telegraph Troop in camp at Blandford, 1872 (above). Airline Wagons on parade (below).

Kent, the troop was moved to Aldershot. The establishment of horses was reduced from 150 to 115, and the move to their new home was completed on 19 August 1871. The new troop continued to take part in local training and to practice both men and horses in the laying out of cable and setting up of telegraph stations in the field.

On 10 August 1872 the troop was split into two 'half-troops' to take part in the large scale manoeuvres due to take place in southern England. One half-troop commenced a march to Blandford on that day with a strength of 2 officers and 108 men, with ". . .2 Offrs horses (and) 80 Troop horses. . . ." The troop reached Blandford by way of Alton, Alresford, Winchester, Romsey and Downton. During the exercise the Southern Army detachment, based at Blandford, laid down a total of 50 miles of cable and during the 28 days of the exercise the telegraph was in use for 370 hours. Faults were frequent and out of the 28 days faults occurred on 26 days but the training proved to be of great value with the men and the horses working well as a team. The greatest length of cable laid out in one day was from Dinton Beeches to Amesbury a distance of 14 miles with the majority of that line being recovered during the same day.

The establishment of the troop was again re-organised in 1873 and then included a Sergeant Farrier, six Shoeing Smiths, 2 Wheelers (wheelwrights) and 92 Drivers, out of a total all rank strength of 234.

The troop was then divided into two, being designated the Right Half-Troop and the Left Half-Troop, and each Half-Troop was sub-divided into two sections. Each section was commanded by a Lieutenant and in 1874 No 1 Section was commanded by Lieutenant H H Kitchener (later to become Field Marshal Earl Kitchener of Khartoum). He departed from the troop on 21 October of that year to take up an appointment in the Palestine Expedition. In the next few years the troop continued to carry out field training without any major changes being made either to the establishment of horses or carriages. The troop had provided a section during the Ashanti War of 1873 but in view of the difficult terrain none of the horses or wagons were sent to the theatre of operations.

C Telegraph Troop was mobilized for active service for the Zulu War of 1879 and Major A C Hamilton (later the 10th Lord Belhaven and Stenton) embarked with half the troop to take part in the campaign. He raised an objection to the fact that he was only permitted to take his 'peace-time' scale of cable with him which only amounted to about 20 miles of wire. The detachment embarked with 7 officers, 200 NCOs and men and 100 horses and provided both telegraph communications and visual signalling during the campaign. On return to the United Kingdom, Major Hamilton was able to convince the War Department that in future the amount of cable to be taken on operations must be based on the known commitment and not on the peace-time scale of holding.

In the remaining years that C Telegraph Troop was to remain in being, which was until 1884, the establishment continued to include the wire wagon, which was not yet referred to as a cable wagon, and the field telegraph office, both being drawn by the troop draught horses.

Whilst the telegraph troop was in barracks the daily training programme of the men of the troop reflected the need to care for the horses that were so much an essential part of troop strength. The following extract from C Troop orders shows this need:

The order was for the trades of Driver and Troop Signaller, during the months of April to October,

Tuesday

6.00 to 7.45am Stables	*8.45 to 10.30am* Driving Drill under OC Troop	*11.00 to 12.30pm* Driving Drill under OC Troop
1.45 to 3.30pm Stables	*3.30 to 4.45pm* School for all below 4th class certificate and voluntary school	*5.00 to 6.00pm* A certain number of men will water and feed horses

The details for other days of the week were of a similar pattern with the emphasis on the care of horses. On Saturday the programme for both drivers and troop signallers was:

6.00 to 7.45am	—	Stables
8.45 to 10.30am	—	Works and Riding Drill
11.00 to 12.30pm	—	Works and Stables
1.45 to 6.00pm	—	Clean up

During 1884 C Telegraph Troop and the former Postal Telegraph Companies were amalgamated to form a Telegraph Battalion RE. C Telegraph Troop became the 1st Division and the two Postal Telegraph Companies formed the 2nd Division, of the Telegraph Battalion RE.

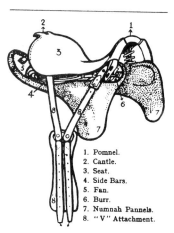

1. Pomnel.
2. Cantle.
3. Seat.
4. Side Bars.
5. Fan.
6. Burr.
7. Numnah Pannels.
8. "V" Attachment.

Saddle showing 'V' attachment.

Chapter 2
Animal Transport in India

The use of mounted messengers was practised in the east from the sixth century when Cyrus of Persia introduced a postal system within the Persian Empire. Having established a distance that a rider and horse would travel during one day a series of stables was established which were then manned by grooms who looked after the horses and ensured that there were always sufficient to supply the needs of the mounted mail service. In the 12th century a similar system was devised by Genghis Khan who controlled a vast empire stretching from Mongolia to the Russian Steppes. In order to keep up-to-date with news from his widely spread territory he established the Mongol Horse Post. The Gobi clansmen were accustomed to ride fifty or sixty miles a day and were ideally suited for the role of mounted messengers. Marco Polo described the system as follows:

> ". . .Now you must know that the messengers of the Emperor travelling from Kambalu find at every twenty five miles of a journey a station they call the Horse Post House. At some of these stations there shall be four hundred horses at others two hundred. Even when the messengers have to pass through a roadless tract where no hostel stands, still the stations are to be found, although at a greater interval . . . in all these posts there are 300,000 horses kept up and the buildings are more than 10,000. In this way, the Emperor receives despatches from places ten days journey off in one day and night. . ."

Each rider carried a gerfalcon tablet which showed that he was on urgent official business and should his horse go lame or otherwise become unfit he was authorised to ". . .dismount whomsoever he may fall in with on the road, and take his horse. . ."

Similar courier systems were used in India throughout the centuries but had virtually vanished by the time that the Honourable East India Company began to take control of the country then known as India.

The introduction of the electric telegraph had reached India and was in use at the time of the Sepoy Mutiny in 1857 but at that time the Honourable East India Company's armies had not introduced the field telegraph system into the army. Although a Signalling School had been set up in Poona in 1872 it only gave instruction on visual signalling as it was considered that the military, when on the move, would not require to know how to operate the electric telegraph system. On 6 January 1875 an order was made to close the School of Army Signalling at Poona and a new establishment was created at Kirkee under the command of Lieutenant H C Selby RE who was at that time appointed 'instructor in Army Signalling'. Training was generally given in the art of visual signalling and with the development of the heliograph there came the need to make the small detachment of heliograph operators mobile and these were then authorised to be mounted. In 1877, Lieutenant G R R Savage, the Inspector of Signalling at Rorkee, commenced the production of heliographs at the regimental workshops. The heliograph was very soon taken into action on the various campaigns on the North West Frontier of India. As a result of the lessons learned during the operations in the South Afghanistan campaign of 1879 and 1880 the following establishment of signallers was recommended for infantry and cavalry brigades:

'..... *Cavalry Brigade* — (with a field force)

One officer and two signallers, all mounted

Infantry Brigade — (two brigades with a field force)

One officer and three signallers .....'

In addition a section was to accompany the headquarter staff which was to consist of an officer and five signallers, all of whom were to be mounted. In addition to the mounts required by the officer and signallers it was necessary to carry the associated signalling equipment and for this purpose each section was authorised to have three pack mules. The recommendation for the loads of each mule was given as follows:

1st mule —	signallers' kits
2nd mule —	tent, cooks' and mule-drivers' kits, head and heel ropes etc, of mules.
3rd mule —	a pair of mule trunks, containing

(1) heliograph and stand
1 telescope and stand
1 Begbie lamp
Small box for 2 Chimneys and 2 mirrors
message pads etc

(2) 2 Bombay deckchies, frypan, rations, with small tins for tea, sugar, etc and, providing it did not contaminate the rations, a tin of kerosene oil.

It was during the Second Afghan War (1878 — 1880) that the first field telegraph train was introduced. Sanction had been sought from the Government for the allocation of stores but this was slow in coming through and was not given until September 1878 on the eve of the outbreak of war in Afghanistan. The train was intended to provide two ground cable detachments and, in keeping with the advances made in the British Army, a proportion of light aerial line was to be included. This 150lbs per mile line was to be suspended on bamboo poles. It was fortunate that the majority of stores had been manufactured at Roorkee, in anticipation of the approval being given.

No 6 Company, Bengal Sappers and Miners had received regular training in the working of the field telegraph train and was therefore ready for active service

Base wire in 40lb coils, with leather wrapping

at the outbreak of the war. The train consisted of three distinct sections, each section having a different method of transportation. The authorised establishment was:

> 2 telegraph offices and 6 miles of cable carried on mules;
> 2 telegraph offices and 12 miles of cable carried on carts;
> 2 telegraph offices and 12 miles of bare wire with poles carried on camels.

The field telegraph train was designed to provide six field telegraph offices and at least 30 miles of line.

The train was given its first taste of active service with the Peshawar Field Force. When 1st Division arrived at Jalalabad it was found that the civil telegraph line had not been installed. The men of the telegraph train went into action and constructed a line from Jalalabad rearwards to Dakka, about 40 miles where it could meet up with the civil line being laid from Peshawar. The ground cable was laid initially as there was a delay in the aerial line stores being brought up to the front. When the stores arrived the line was supplemented by the aerial line which was constructed on the bamboo poles. The ground line worked from 25 January to 10 February and the aerial line from that date until 10 March 1879

Alternative method of carrying cable

and during this time more than 3,300 messages were passed along the line. On 10 March the civil line reached Jalalabad and the military line was recovered for further use when required. It was seen that the field telegraph office was a success and that the line laying was more than adequate.

One report recorded that:

> ". . .The Sappers commenced an overhead line directly the troops moved and with a rapidity which reflects great credit on their construction, the office getting into Gandamak the same time as the advance guard. . . ."

The Madras Sappers and Miners were also to receive some active service with their field telegraph train when it was despatched to Egypt in 1882 to join the expeditionary force at Suez. The train, which was a section of E Company, consisted of telegraphists, with their equipment, plus ten miles of cable to be carried on mule transport. The train provided valuable service to the divisional headquarters and the force headquarters.

In 1885 a reorganisation of the Sapper and Miner Corps took place and a Depot Company was formed in each of the Corps. Bengal and Madras Corps were authorised to establish two telegraph sections each, and A Company of the Bombay Sappers and Miners was authorised to have one telegraph section. The telegraph sections were established to have 4 British NCOs and 18 Indian soldiers who

Load of tools, shovels, crow bars etc.

Mule carrying office equipment.

Load of poles, each pole in 3 pieces. Each mule carried ½ mile of poles.

were all to be trained to carry out line construction work. These sections were also established to have animals included on their strength and in India this could mean either, horses, mules, camels and in some cases elephants.

Elephants were used in Assam and Burma and the care of them was in accordance with the instructions issued by the Posts and Telegraphs Department of India. The regulations issued by the army did not generally cover the care of elephants. The instructions give quite specific detail on the care of the animal by the mahout and includes such special information such as feeding:

". . . .each animal should be given 8 tubbees of paddy daily
with a handful, say 10 tickels, of white salt and great
care should be taken that they get sufficient fodder, as
each animal needs as much as 15 maunds of green fodder
daily. Food should be given early so that the animals
may have sufficient time to fill their stomachs and then
have about 4 hours sleep. Between half a pound and a

Poles in two pieces, for two miles of airline.

pound each of tamarind and salt should be given to each
animal once every ten days. . . --- a little coconut oil
should be applied over the forehead every other day. . . ."
In addition to the feeding the regulations gave details of load and working hours
giving the following specific instructions:

". . .Elephants should be ready to start very early in the
morning and no work should be given between 11.30am and
2.30pm. When carrying loads of wire or posts, the animals
should be relieved of their loads for an hour or so half-
way.
Elephants should be bathed twice a day, once before 8am
and again between 3 and 4pm. When bathing, they should
be scrubbed with a piece of over-burnt brick or some
such thing. . . ."

The two illustrations show two elephants loaded with line construction
equipment, one carrying two-piece bamboo poles for the air-line, the amount

Elephant with wire howdah, (Not fully loaded)

carried would suffice for a two mile line. The second illustration shows a wire dispenser in a howdah but does not include the normal load of wire that would be carried.

When not on active service all elephants were given a full day's rest and should any animal fall ill or become weak the orders gave instructions that the animal should not be given any work.

The other animals used by the field telegraph sections such as horses, ponies, mules, bullocks, and camels were all governed by army regulations and these cover a whole range of subject matters including the registration of animals.

In general all animals were to be registered and taken 'on charge' of their parent unit and annual returns submitted. The regulations state that:

> ''. . .for the purpose of reports and returns the year of the age of every animal will be reckoned from 1st April with the exception of imported Australian horses whose ages will be reckoned from 1st October. . .''

The regulations also cover procedures for obtaining replacement animals; the

A 'Column camp' during the Third Afghan War, 1919 – Note horse lines in foreground.

2nd Indian Divisional Signals on the King Emperor's Birthday Parade at Quetta, 1928, with 2 telegraph Wagons. 2GS limber wagons and 2 cable wagons.

A cable wagon detachment in India, circa 1932.

Animal power comes to the aid of the Royal Air Force
on the North West frontier of India, 1933

arrival of animals in units, and the method to be adopted for the branding of military animals. The regulation stated that:

> ". . .all animals on receipt by units will be branded with the unit serial number as follows:
>
> Horses, ponies and mules   —   on the fore feet
> Bullocks   —   on the horns
> Camels   —   on the near neck. . ."

The types of animal used by the Indian Army remained virtually unchanged throughout the latter part of the 19th century and during the period leading up to the First World War. There were, during this time, frequent periods of conflict on the North West Frontier and horses, mules and camels employed by the field telegraph sections were fully used in the laying and recovery of field telephone cable.

The Soldiers' Pocket Book published in 1874 gives details of the suitability of various animals that were in use in the army in addition to the horse.

The first listed was the mule which was shown as being almost a rival to the horse in usefulness for general military purposes. The load was given as being 200 to 250lbs including the pack saddle and the height of the service mule was between 13 to 16 hands.

The bullock was also shown as being ". . . admirable for slow draught over rough roads . . . or other places where there are no roads at all. . ." The instruction continued by saying that they should not be hurried and that their ordinary pace was from 2 to 2½ miles an hour. The bullock was considered to be at its prime at 6 years of age and it was also observed that ". . . they want but little care, and thrive well on poor food . . ."

Two other animals were referred to in the instruction, these being the camel, which is dealt with in Chapter 4, and the elephant.

The elephant was considered to be fit for work at 20 years of age and would last to 50 or even 60 years of age. The normal load for an elephant was given as being between 15 to 20cwt and that on the march they would be expected to travel from 3 to 3½ miles an hour.

Thus the range of animals on a permanent basis within the army in India was the horse, pony, mule, bullock, camel and elephant.

As with officers and soldiers occurrences affecting an animal on the strength of the unit was promulgated in the unit Part II Orders, an example can be seen at page 28. This shows that one horse and two mules had been admitted to the Military Veterinary Hospital at Jubbulpore (now known as Jabalpur) and one horse and one pack mule had been discharged from the hospital.

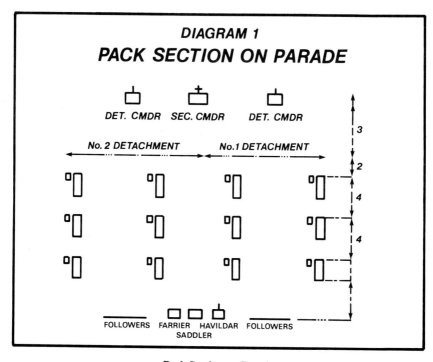

Pack Section on Parade.

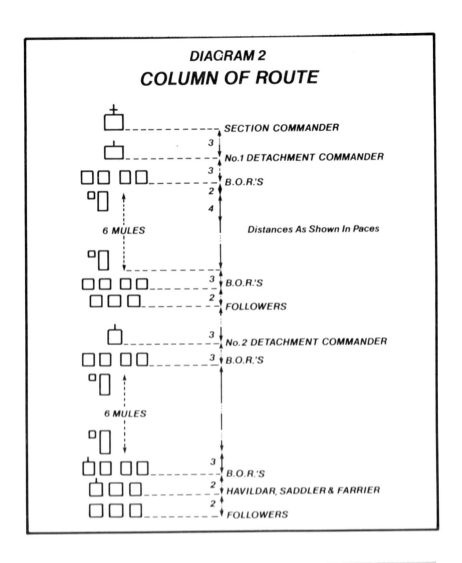

DIAGRAM 2
COLUMN OF ROUTE

SECTION COMMANDER

3

No.1 DETACHMENT COMMANDER

3

B.O.R.'S

2

4

6 MULES

Distances As Shown In Paces

3 B.O.R.'S

2 FOLLOWERS

3 No.2 DETACHMENT COMMANDER

3 B.O.R.'S

6 MULES

3 B.O.R.'S

2 HAVILDAR, SADDLER & FARRIER

2 FOLLOWERS

The use of pack animals was generally covered by locally produced instructions. No 2 Wireless Section, of A Corps Signals, based at Karachi, produced a printed handbook "Notes on Pack and Light Motor Sections". This instruction gave details of loads for each animal, and yakdan, and also a diagram showing the position of men and animals on parade (See Page 26) and on the line of march .

PART II ORDERS.

BY

Major. A.W. ROBERTS, M.C. R. Signals,
Offg. Commanding, Signal Training Battalion, S.T.C. (I).

BRITISH OFFICERS.

277 STRENGTH - DECREASE.

Captain J.F. Maxwell, A.I R.O.

Appointed to the Mewar Bhil Corps for duty and proceeded to Kherwara on 11th. June, 1932, (afternoon). Struck of the strength of the S.T.C. (I). w.e.f. that date, Authy:- A.H.Q. (I) M.S. Branch No.05010/198 dated 1/6/32).

278 SICK IN QUARTERS LIST.

Lieut R.M Adams, R. Signals

Struck off the 'Sick in Quarters List' w.e f. 7/6/32.

BRITISH OTHER RANKS.

279 DEATHS.

2306293 CQMS. Francis H.E.

Died at Jubbulpore on 7-6-1932. Cause of death-Heat Stroke.

280 BIRTHS.

1850271 CSM Bew G J.

Daughter born at British Families Hospital, Jubbulpore, on 6-6-32.

281 EDUCATIONAL AWARDS.

| 2312799 Sjt. Marchant | E. | Urdu. | Passed in subjects stated towards the Army Special Certificate of Education at an examination held in Jubbulpore on 23-3-32 (Deccan District Order 519/1932). |
| 2308511 ,, Gregory | G. | Maths. B. | |

ANIMALS.

283 HOSPITAL-ADMISSIONS & DISCHARGES.

One charger, (over 15 hands), property of Capt.J.Wynn. ... 4. 6. 32
L. D, Mule 42 ... 4. 6. 32.
Pack Mule 27 ... 6. 5, 32.

Admitted M.V.H. Jubbulpore on dates shown and struck off ration strength accordingly.

Horse No. 47 ... 8. 6.32.
Pack Mule 27 ... 8. 6.32.

Discharged M.V.H. Jubbulpore on dates shown and taken on ration strength accordingly.

(Sd.) W.F. HERDON, Captain R. Signals.
Adjutant, Signal Training Battalion,
Signal Training Centre, (India.)

Chapter 3
The Cable Wagon and Cable Cart

With the formation of the Telegraph Battalion RE in 1884 the establishment of officers and men increased, as did the amount of authorised equipment, but little change was made to the means of transportation in the field. The 1869 'wire wagon' had changed little except that it was now referred to as the 'cable wagon' and this line laying vehicle was pulled by a team of six horses as can be seen in the illustration which shows the cable wagon at camp in the New Forest, near Brockenhurst in 1890. The 1st Telegraph Battalion left Aldershot on 19 May and marched to Brockenhurst via Winchester. The Record of Service compiled by Major C F C Beresford, shows that ''. . . 8 officers, 215 NCOs and men (including 27 boys) and 104 horses with 21 vehicles, viz 7 air-line wagons, 2 cable wagons, 3 cable carts, 6 general service wagons, 1 forage cart, and 2 water carts. . .'' moved out to the summer camp.

Included in the convoy were 3 cable carts, which were then in use and were considered to be faster than the cable wagon. The cart was pulled by two horses with the rider mounted on the left hand horse of the pair. The illustration at page 38 also shows the outrider who was an essential part of the line laying detachment. The camp proved to be successful with men being trained in cable and air-line laying in the New Forest area covering routes to such places as Hurst Castle on the southern coast and to Hythe and to Netley, across Southampton Water.

Later in the year the unit took part in the Cavalry Manoeuvres which were held on the Berkshire Downs. The battalion was required to provide communications for the exercise and on 6 September 1890 the unit moved out of Aldershot with 6 officers, 1 Medical officer, and 138 NCOs and men. The transport provided on this occasion was to be drawn by 48 draught horses, and in addition there were 18 riding horses and 9 officers' horses. The transport consisted of 4 air-line wagons, 3 cable wagons, 3 cable carts, 3 G.S. wagons, 1 water cart and 1 experimental cart which was really an adaption of the Irish cart which was drawn by a single horse. The illustration shows the cart with the men on the side seats and with the air-line poles protruding from the rear of the car. The report on the exercise showed that the telegraph detachments had worked well and it recorded the following rates of line construction of field telegraph lines:

	Open Country	Enclosed Country
Air line	1½ to 2 miles per hour	½ to 1 mile per hour
Cable, with same detachment laying and arranging for crossings etc	2 to 3 miles per hour	1 to 2 miles per hour

The Cable Wagon, circa 1890.

Major Beresford experimental cart for fast cable laying.

Cable, fast work with cable carts, with small detachments following in light carts to arrange crossings etc	3 to 6 miles per hour	3 to 6 miles per hour

The work of the follow-up party when using the third system of line laying called for a degree of improvisation when fixing the line for road crossings etc and the illustration at page 34 shows one of the linesmen using his horse as a means of reaching the top of the air-line pole.

The equipment of the telegraph unit remained virtually unchanged until the commencement of the South African War brought the unit into active service. The Telegraph Battalion proved to be a great asset to the General Staff and in one instance General French, who was opposing the advance of the Boers in the Colesberg area, directed his flank formations by telegraph using airline and cable and was able to give direct orders to the artillery which gave him a decisive victory.

The experimental 'Fast' cable cart, circa 1890.

Lance Corporal J Collier at exercise camp at Arundel, 1893, in 'Parade Dress'.

Cable cart, 1893. Showing positions of linesmen when reeling up.

Lineman improving the line on exercise during 1897

He attributed his success to the work of the telegraph sections working with his headquarters.

Not all commanders were as appreciative of the mobile field telegraph service and some preferred to rely upon the Army Signal Service which was a visual and messenger organisation which worked as a rival to the telegraph organisation rather than with it. Captain E. G. Godfrey-Faussett and his cable cart was the first detachment of any arm to enter Bloemfontein but unfortunately the air-line was 'down' behind him and he was unable to communicate. Lord Roberts sent his victory signal by mounted messenger from the Army Signal Service. However the Telegraph Section discovered an indirect line to Kimberley which was only slightly damaged and Lieutenant (later Sir Harry) Mackworth and Sergeant C. Cadwell, galloped out and repaired the line. When their horses were tired they

Telegraph Battalion linesmen in South Africa, 1900.

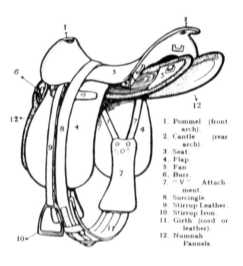

1. Pommel (front arch).
2. Cantle (rear arch).
3. Seat.
4. Flap.
5. Fan.
6. Burr.
7. "V" Attachment.
8. Surcingle.
9. Stirrup Leather.
10. Stirrup Iron.
11. Girth (cord or leather).
12. Numnah Pannels.

Saddle complete.

Cable cart of the 1st Division, Telegraph Battalion, 1st Army Corps, at Edenburg, Orange River Colony, 1901. The detachment consisted of Lieutenant Lawson, Sergeant Salter, Corporal Peerless, 2nd Corporal Cole, Sappers, Gleeson, Dickinson, Snow, Kempster, Fell and four locally enlisted black South Africans.

replaced them by acquiring new mounts from Boer laagers at night and by the following evening the line was through to Kimberley and the message passed three hours before the arrival of the mounted orderly.

The following illustration shows the cable cart in action during the South African War. The telegraph sections worked extremely hard during the war and the Guerrilla War that followed which lasted from 1900 to 1902. During the whole conflict 9,360 miles of line were erected and nearly two thousand telephones taken into use. Altogether during the whole war some 18,000 miles of line had been laid and 28,000 miles maintained. It had been proved that communications were now an essential part of any army.

Following the end of the war in South Africa the Telegraph Battalion was re-organised in 1905 and the Companies became independent. In the following year the Evelyn Wood Committee recommended that the telegraph units and the Signal Service should combine so as to provide all forms of communication from regimental and battalion level back to base. In 1908 the recommendations were accepted and, rather than form a new Corps at that time, the Royal Engineer Signal Service was formed.

During this transitional period the actual telegraph companies continued to provide the line communications for the divisions. In 1907 the re-organisation, which was authorised from 15 April, saw the formation of the following companies:

	Qty
Air-Line Telegraph Company —	2
Cable Telegraph Company —	2
Divisional Telegraph Company —	6

and at this time two Wireless Telegraph Companies were also created.

The actual equipment for each independent company was authorised as follows:

Air-Line Telegraph Company
". . . personnel for eight detachments to erect air-line, maintenance staff for about 160 miles of line, and staff for sixteen telegraph offices. . ." The equipment was carried on sixteen air-line wagons, and four cable wagons. However in peace time the whole establishment was reduced by half.

Cable Telegraph Company
". . .personnel for eight cable detachments. It carries sixty-four miles of cable and sixteen office sets in eight cable wagons; also sixteen additional miles of cable and eight spare office sets in eight light wagons. . ." In peace time this establishment was also reduced both in men and horses to provide only four detachments.

The Divisional Telegraph Company was equipped with two cable carts and a forage wagon.

In the same year, 1907, a War Office instruction was issued giving details of 'Laying and Maintaining Field Telegraph Lines' and in this pamphlet the duties

The Cable Cart in South Africa.

Drawing by I Sheldon-Williams.

38

of cable-wagon team are given as follows:

> ". . . The cable wagon has a 4-horse team with 2 drivers.
> An officer or non-commissioned officer, mounted, commander.
> 2 office telegraphists, dismounted, Nos 1 and 2.
> 3 sappers, dismounted, Nos 3, 4 and 5.
> 2 linemen, mounted Nos 6 and 7 . . ."

Thus each detachment had a total of seven horses. The men, Nos 1 to 5, travelled on the cable wagon. The four horse cable wagon continued to be used until the start of the First World War when the team was generally increased to six horses, still with the commander and the two linemen as out-riders.

With the development of the Territorial Force the volunteer telegraph units were also equipped with the cable wagon and initially also with the cable cart. The illustration shows a Territorial cable laying detachment with a cable cart in 1910. It was during the following year, 1911, that the cable cart was taken out of service and all line laying detachments were then equipped with the cable wagon.

The cable wagon saw active service during the First World War and all the annual training that had taken place during the years leading up to that conflict proved of great value. During the years, from the reorganisation of the Telegraph Battalions into the Royal Engineers Signal Service, all detachments were continually laying line on both local and command exercises, and the training and experience gained were put to good use in France. Cable wagons were used during the war to great effect as they were able to provide lines quickly and efficiently. The line could be laid at speed and it was possible to provide line communications for a division even when that division was on the move.

There was, however, a gradual move from horse-drawn transport towards motorised transport. The Cable Section commenced the war in 1914 with an establishment of 2 cable-wagons and in 1918 still had the same establishment of cable wagons but the Airline Section lost its one cable wagon on the establishment by the end of the war, and was then equipped with two 30-cwt lorries and a 15-cwt Box car. In addition to the cable wagon being withdrawn from its establishment it had also had the 2 airline wagons and the 2 light wagons removed from the establishment. It had, in fact, ceased to have animals on its establishment.

The cable wagon was used to good effect in the campaign in Mesopotamia where it was manned by the men of the Indian Signals and the illustration depicts a cable laying team in action with the linemen riding in the rear of the wagon.

As a result of the work of the Royal Engineer Signal Service during the war it was decided by the War Office that a separate Corps should be formed to provide communications within the army. The Corps of Signals was formed on 28 June 1920, by the authority of the Sovereign, and six weeks later His Majesty King George V conferred the title 'Royal' on the Corps which was effective from 5th August 1920.

The newly-formed Corps set up a Signal Training Centre at Maresfield and during the years that followed the linemen of the Corps continued to be trained in the skills of line laying by use of the six-horse cable wagon. The Signal Training Manual, Part IV, which dealt with Line Telegraphy and Telephony, and published

A Cable Cart Detachment from the Territorial Army on exercise, 1910.

The Airline Wagon at Rowlands Castle, 1910. The wagon was known by the detachment as 'the hearse'.

The Cable Wagon on exercise in 1911.

42

Watercolour by unknown artist showing pack cable laying, with linesmen in Full Dress, at Aldershot during a Royal Visit, 1912.

Men of the Limerick Signal Company watering horses whilst on exercise in Ireland, 1912.

An Airtline Wagon in Ireland, circa 1913.

Cable Wagon in Mesopotamia, 1917.

46

Indian Lineman on patrol, Mesopotamia, 1917.

The Cable Wagon on active service during the First World War. The Cable Wagon was introduced into service under the authority of Army Order dated 1 July 1907.

in 1922, gave the revised organisation of a cable wagon detachment. The team consisted of:

". . . One NCO mounted as a commander.
Two signalmen, dismounted, Nos 1 and 2.
Three linemen, dismounted, Nos 3, 4 and 5.
Three linemen, mounted, Nos 6, 7 and 8 . . ."

The cable wagon had a six-horse team with three drivers, and was accompanied by a 'wagon, limbered RE' which had a pair of horses and a driver. The limbered wagon carried the extra cable, spares and rations for the detachment. The instructions gave the following:

". . . Every man of the detachment will carry a knife, pliers, and some lengths of spunyarn. In addition the following will be carried:

Commander	—	Crookstick and whistle
No 4	—	Whistle
No 6	—	Whistle, 100 yard length of cable, two pieces of tubing, two pegs, mattock in case, and crookstick.
Nos 7 and 8	—	100 yards length of cable, two pieces of tubing, two pegs, mattock in case and crookstick.

One of the detachment — preferably No 3 — should be detailed as wagonman. His duties are to be responsible that the wagon and its equipment are complete in all parts and in good order . . ."

The men of the detachment were permitted to store their rolled coats on the limber, and their accoutrements, except the bandolier which had to be worn, could be stored on the wagon ". . . in places previously arranged by the detachment commander. . ."

The cable wagon, and of course the out-riding horse, continued to be used by the Corps until 1937 when they were replaced by a new mechanised force. However the passing of the cable wagon and the mounted line laying detachments is marked within the Corps by a painting of a Cable Detachment by A. E. Haswell Miller, MC, RSW, and by a silver centrepiece which shows in great detail the complete detachment including the out-riders.

The continued use of the horse in connection with the various line laying wagons and carts and the out riders from the formation of C Telegraph Troop in 1870 until its demise, as a means of line laying, in 1937 ensured that there was always a close affiliation between the men of the various Troops, Companies etc and the horses that were part of the establishment.

As will have been seen the horses were of paramount importance and their care and well being was very much part of the daily life of the men of the line laying detachments.

Included in the Standing Orders for Signal Units due consideration was given to stable duties as well as the normal duties required within the barracks, or camp, for the mess room, billets and ablutions. The following is the order written by Lieutenant F R Cobb, RE for the Company stables in Egypt in 1913:

Horse lines

". . .STABLE ORDERLY:-

His duties will commence at reveille when he will take over the horse stables, its equipment etc in charge of the Signals Units from the night guard of the Cavalry Regiment.

He will remain in or about the stable during his tour of duty except during the following hours when he may go to the Signals Unit for meals.

    1 hour for breakfast

    12.30 to 1.30pm

    4.30 to 5.00pm

During his tour of duty he will be responsible for the horse stables equipment, he will see that the stalls are swept out by the natives. He will see that no unauthorised natives loiter about the stables.

If any horse gets sick or any accident occurs he will send the horse to the Veterinary Hospital.

He will not smoke whilst on duty.

He will come off duty when he is relieved by the night guard of the Cavalry Regiment. . ."

The affection that developed between the men of the line laying detachments and the horses is well illustrated by the story of 'Nobby', horse number '30091'. 'Nobby' was purchased out of the service at the age of 24, in 1934 by all ranks of 1st Divisional Signals. He had served throughout the First World War in France and was an expert in a cable wagon team and doubled as a riding horse. He was

'Nobby'
— the retired cable horse bought by the soldiers of 1st Divisional Signals.

given the freedom of Mons Barracks, and attended all functions such as Sergeants' Mess Dinners and NAAFI breaks. Mechanisation caused his final retirement to a farm paddock in 1937.

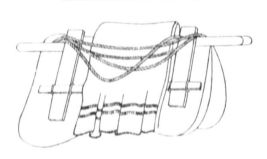

Methods of loading camel and driver's gear.

Cable Wagon in Danzig in 1919.   (Courtesy of Major T Fortescue-Hitchin).

The Cable Wagon on exercise in Southern England during the 1930s.

A line detachment at work. (Courtesy of the Army Museum and Ogilby Trust).

54

A Cable Wagon of 56th (London) Divisional Signals in the 1930 Lord Mayor's Procession.

A Cable Wagon of City of London Signals reeling in during Easter training near Aldershot in 1936.

The Cable Wagon without a full detachment.

(above) An Indian Cable Wagon detachment.

(below) The last mounted parade of 'B' Cable Section of 2nd Divisional Signals on 26 February 1937.

The Cable Wagon stripped down for the last Aldershot Tattoo before the outbreak of the Second World War.

Camel carrying line equipment in Palestine, 1916.

60

Chapter 4
Camels and Communications

Although the camel had been used in India for the carriage of the stores, the most effective use of camels, in large numbers, took place during the 1903 campaign when the Somaliland Field Force was formed. A Telegraph section which had been formed from the officers and men of the 1st Division, Telegraph Battalion, Royal Engineers left England on 2 January 1903. The section consisted of 2 officers and 58 NCOs and men and arrived at Berbera on 23 January. On 31 January it was ordered to proceed to lay a landline to Bohote. The party, led by Lieutenant Mackworth, consisted of :

> 45 NCOs and men
> 33 native muleteers
> 58 mules
> 50 Government camels) borrowed for the
> 26 camel drivers　　　) expedition.

The report written dealing with the problems encountered showed that initially there had been difficulty with the loading of the camels. The report reads:

> ". . .There was at first some difficulty in getting the poles on to camels; 40 poles (2 bundles of 10 on each side) were loaded on to one camel. This, with the type of saddle used by Somali camels, made an awkward load, but the camels managed to do it. With the alternate heavy dew and heat, the spunyard with which the bundles of poles were tied rotted, and with subsequent loads of poles it was found necessary to cut the short 8ft poles into two to form cradles, and to load the camels with two bundles of 16 poles, fastened tightly by wire. . ."

Dealing with the actual maintenance of the line, the report showed that the camel was more preferable to the mule in the type of country in which the Field Force was operating.

The report reads:

> ". . .For maintaining the line, linemen are provided with mules; although they did well enough, there is no doubt that riding camels, or at least a good proportion of them, should be used in a future campaign under similar circumstances. On a riding camel a lineman can carry all he wants for two or three days, whereas with a mule he had to carry water for it as well, and could seldom stay a night out. . ."

The recommendation also suggested that each officer should be supplied with two riding camels.

During the campaign 432 miles of air line was erected and 504 miles of cable laid. The cable cart was used during the campaign but this could only be used

Camel carrying line equipment in the Sudan.

in a very limited area as the terrain precluded the use of this type of transport and therefore the camel and mule transport proved to be more efficient.

The Soldier's Pocket Book For Field Service, which was written by Major General Sir Garnet J Wolseley, in 1874, contains the following notes on the use of camels by the military:

> ". . .Camels are used in the East from 3 to 16 years of age; about 7 ft high (to top of hump), about 8 ft long from nose to tail. Pace about 2 miles an hour, kept up steadily for the longest marches; load for service about 400 to 450lbs. . ."

He also comments that the camel will thrive well upon leaves of trees and can go without water longer than any other animal, and that they are admirably suited to carrying long articles, such as scaling ladders etc. Certainly within the Telegraph Sections the camel did perform well carrying both line ladders and air line poles. The illustrations show the camel in use in the Sudan and also in the Mesopotamia campaign of the First World War where it is shown carrying line poles.

Camels in use for transportation of radio equipment in South Arabia, circa 1966.

Royal Signals personnel serving with the Federation Regular Army, South Arabia, 1965. Radios being used on camels and in Land Rovers.

As can be seen from the two previous illustrations, camels are still used as a means of transport in the Middle East and Persian Gulf areas and are quite capable of carrying heavy radio equipment. Radio sets can be loaded on to an adapted harness, together with batteries, so that a mobile working set can be taken into remote areas which are often inaccessible to motorised transport.

Chapter 5
The Advent of Wireless

The war in South Africa brought about a new development in communications and one which was to have a far reaching effect on the future of the Telegraph Battalion. In 1895-96 Marconi was experimenting with wireless and in 1898 the English Channel was spanned. The Royal Engineer Committee appointed Captain J. N. C. Kennedy to monitor the progress being made by the Marconi Company. In the same year it was decided to hire, from the Marconi Company, a 'wireless system', complete with operators for active service in South Africa. Whilst Captain Kennedy and his party of Sappers and Marconi operators were on their way to South Africa it was decided that the wireless should be used for mobile communications. Mr. Bullocke, the senior Marconi representative in the party, agreed that the set would probably provide the type of communication that was expected. On arrival at Cape Town time was spent building the set into G S wagons. The experiments at Cape Town were successful and then it was found that not only were the unsprung wagons unsuitable for the carriage of wireless equipment but the Marconi masts were too bulky and the Siemens masts, that had been found in the Customs shed and which had originally been intended for the Boers, were too complicated. It was decided that 30 foot bamboos would be used instead and these were taken up country. The wireless sets were transferred to the Australian pattern spring-wagon and moved out to De Aar, Modder, Enslin, Belmont and the Orange River. The use of wireless during the war, and the Guerrilla War that followed, was never very successful and this new medium of communications was not universally accepted at this time.

It was during the reorganisation of 1907 that the Royal Engineer Signal Service received two new companies on its establishment and these were solely committed to wireless communication. Both the Regular and Territorial force units were equipped with wireless carts in 1908 and the carts were required to carry telescopic masts as well as the actual wireless set. In 1912 the first wireless course was set up and with this means of communication making progress the equipment was continually being modified and improved, and as a result the wireless wagon was evolved from the wireless cart. Both were horse drawn and the wireless sections had, in addition to the wireless operators, drivers on their establishment for the wagons. By the outset of the First World War the wireless section had been motorised and had lost its establishment of horses.

Although the carriage of wireless equipment changed from animal drawn transport to mechanised transport in Europe this was not the case in many of the overseas stations and in particular India.

The C Set which was in general use in India was carried by either mules or pack ponies. The report of the operations on the North West Frontier in 1924 contains the following detail:

".... On 1 June 1924 the Razmak Moveable Column of a strong mixed brigade organised with pack transport made its first promenade out of Razmak. The Razmak Brigade (Signals) Section with the Pack Cable

Wireless limbered wagons, carrying telescopic masts, c. 1911.

The Wireless Set mounted in a Wireless Wagon.

Marconi transportable spare wireless sets in light spring wagons, c1914

Section and Wireless Section accompanied the column with a strength of 100 other ranks and 45 animals. . ."

The column was about five miles long and the transport was provided by a very large number of mules, camels and carts all of which were used to carry equipment and supplies for the column.

The pack animals on the establishment of the Indian Signals units were required to carry not only the sets but also the generator. This type of transport for the wireless sets continued throughout the 1920's but in 1925 it was decided that the C Set, which had replaced the Marconi half kilowatt spark set and had been designed for carriage on pack mules at a walk, should be adapted so that it could be carried on a pack horse which travelled at a fast pace in order that it could keep up with the cavalry whilst out on column.

A pack wireless section consisted of three sets which required frequent practice by the signallers to ensure that the sets could be erected and dismantled without undue delay. All the mules of the section had to be put through a training programme and it was essential that any mule that disliked carrying his load had to receive additional training. The wireless sets were fragile and replacements and spare parts were difficult to obtain. If a mule showed a tendency to try to kick off its load it was normally given two hours 'pack drill'. This meant going round and round a parade ground with a heavy load of sandbags on its back in lieu of the wireless set. This additional training was given during the afternoon

No 1 set detachment, 2nd Cavalry Brigade Signal Troop. Sialkot, India.

No 1 Set detachment in India.

when it was extremely hot and it was said that two successive days of this type of training usually subdued even the most obstinate mule. Of course the unfortunate soldier also had to attend the training and was equally as keen to ensure that the mule settled into the routine of carrying pack wireless sets.

In addition to the actual wireless sets, the mules, or pack ponies, were required to carry all the other stores needed by the section and it was for this purpose that the yakdan was brought into use.

The military yakdan was a version of the panniers used for many centuries by traders in the hill regions of India, particularly the Himalayas and over the borders in the Hindu Kush and Tibet, for carrying their goods as side-loads on Yaks and ponies, and which are still in use today.

This military type came into general use in the Indian Army early this century, and was in full use until the Second World War, when it became largely redundant as a result of mechanisation. It was particularly useful to the Indian Signal Corps for carrying their Wireless sets and gear in two loads, each up to 80lbs, one on each side of a pack pony or mule. pack ponies or horses were preferred for this role as giving the 'smoother ride' for the wireless sets and which were faster than mules and could keep up with the (horsed) Cavalry.

70

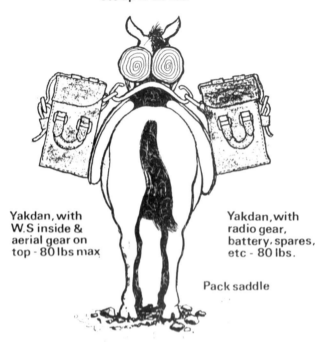

'top hamper'
usually bedding
etc up to 20 lbs.

Yakdan, with
W.S inside &
aerial gear on
top - 80 lbs max

Yakdan, with
radio gear,
battery, spares,
etc - 80 lbs.

Pack saddle

TOTAL MAX LOAD 180 lbs

There were however experiments being carried out with mechanised cable laying equipment and with wireless sets installed in vehicles. In April 1930 a new establishment was taken into use by A and B Corps Signals in India which included both animal and mechanised transport. The establishment included the following:

Horses	52	Motor cycles	20
Mules	16	Cars, vans and lorries	47

The unit however retained four cable wagons.

During the 1933 Mount Everest expedition two members of the Royal Corps of Signals, Lieutenant E. C. Thompson (later killed in Malaya whilst serving as a Colonel) and Lieutenant W. R. Smijth-Windham (subsequently Brigadier W. R. Smijth-Windham, CBE DSO ADC FRGS), accompanied the party to provide wireless communication back to civilization. The wireless equipment was transported by mule and pony transport and this alone amounted to eleven loads.

No 1 Set, with operator on left with wrist morse key.

No I Set, North West Frontier, India.

The wireless and line equipment had to be transported to the base camps and in later stages some of the equipment had to be carried by Yak. (See illustration at page 76).

By 1937 animal transport had virtually ceased to exist for the carriage of wireless in India except in the North West Frontier area where it was still necessary to use mule and pack pony to reach some of the more remote areas.

There was one notable exception when, in 1938, the No I wireless set was used mounted in howdahs on the back of elephants and used in connection with crowd control duties. This had an obvious advantage in such a situation as it permitted the operator to see over the heads of the vast crowds and enabled him to keep in touch with the other members of his section.

The horse was still very much a part of everyday life in India, even after mechanisation with officers and men taking part in equestrian events and joining various hunts that had been established in India. As late as 1946 British other ranks were still encouraged to learn to ride and to take an interest in the care and well being of horses and ponies which had, by this time, generally become unit private property.

No 1 set detachment on the move.

Indian Signal Corps units – 1935

Headquarters units	Station
Army Headquarters staff	Delhi
Northern Command	Rawalpindi — Murree
Western Command	Quetta
Eastern Command	Naini Tal
Southern Command	Poona

Units	Station
A Corps Signals	Rawalpindi
B Corps Signals	Karachi
1st Indian Divisional Signals	Rawalpindi
2nd Indian Divisional Signals	Quetta
3rd Indian Divisional Signals	Meerut
4th Indian Divisional Signals	Trimulgherry
1st Cavalry Brigade Signal Troop	Risalpur
2nd Cavalry Brigade Signal Troop	Sialkot

SIGNAL UNIT
STATIONS
IN INDIA
1920-1938

3rd Cavalry Brigade Signal Troop	Meerut
4th Cavalry Brigade Signal Troop	Secunderabad
Kohat District Signals	Kohat
Peshawar District Signals	Peshawar
Waziristan District Signals	Dera Ismail Khan
W/T Experimental Section	Quetta
Zhob Signal Section	Loralai
Signal Training Centre	Jubbulpore
Signal Training School	Jubbulpore
Army Signal School	Poona

Signal equipment being carried on a Yak for the Mount Everest expedition, 1933.

C Set in use on the Wana Column, c 1934.

Corporal Donaghy with a No 1 Set on the North West Frontier, 1937.

No I set – Pack horse mounted for use by Indian Cavalry Brigade Signal Troops.

550 Watt charging engine, on pack horses, India, 1937

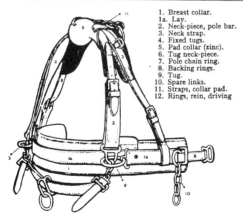

1. Breast collar.
1a. Lay.
2. Neck-piece, pole bar.
3. Neck strap.
4. Fixed tugs.
5. Pad collar (zinc).
6. Tug neck-piece.
7. Pole chain ring.
8. Backing rings.
9. Tug.
10. Spare links.
11. Straps, collar pad.
12. Rings, rein, driving

Breast Collar, neck strap and neck-piece pole bar.

80

Pack 'C' Set detachment. North West Frontier, 1937

No 1 Set providing 'Press' communications at Kadir, 1937

No 1 Set on crowd control duty in India. 1938

Pack animal carrying a Wireless Set No 22

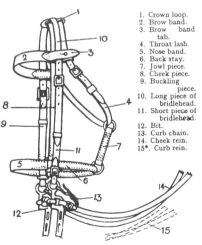

1. Crown loop.
2. Brow band.
3. Brow band tab.
4. Throat lash.
5. Nose band.
6. Back stay.
7. Jowl piece.
8. Cheek piece.
9. Buckling piece.
10. Long piece of bridlehead.
11. Short piece of bridlehead.
12. Bit.
13. Curb chain.
14. Cheek rein.
15*. Curb rein.

Head collar with bit and bridlehead.

Chapter 6
Messenger Dogs

In 1916 Lieutenant Colonel E. H. Richardson was asked by the War Office to set up an official dog training school but this was only after repeated applications by the Colonel for his ideas to be adopted. He was convinced that, with many messengers being killed on the front line, a dog would be able to perform this duty if trained properly. It would certainly provide a much more difficult target to the enemy snipers and he felt that a trained dog would be able to perform other duties as well as just carry messages.

The Germans had dogs working in their army from the very beginning of the war. They had carried out experimental work with dogs since 1870 and had organised a network of village clubs which trained dogs for army work so that when war was declared they had a ready made 'service' available for their army. The British passion for keeping dogs as pets, or as gun-dogs, precluded such a scheme within the United Kingdom. Even had it been suggested no-one would have wanted to part with their dog on the outbreak of war.

Colonel Richardson and his wife set up a training school at Shoeburyness and commenced training dogs for their war time duties. The dogs were trained to return to their handler and were conditioned to ignore rifle fire, shell fire and to get through such obstacles as barbed wire. The dogs were taken out from their kennel and once released would make their way home to their handler and would then be rewarded with food. They were also trained to pass troops firing over their heads, through smoke barrages and to pass through riflemen in extended line firing volleys towards the enemy.

Unfortunately the good record of message-carrying dogs was marred by the kindness of the British troops in the front line who were inclined to treat them as pets rather than a means of passing messages. The standard work on the history of the Royal Engineer Signal Service, during 1914 to 1919, gives no mention of the use of dogs within the service, although contemporary illustrations show that dogs were used by the Signal Service. The following illustrations depict dogs with their handlers in France.

A small number of dogs were also trained to carry a small cable dispenser on their back and to cross areas laying out field cable as they went. This method could only be used for short distances, such as from one front line to another due to the small size of the dispenser pack. This method was only used in a few isolated cases and was never continued after the end of the First World War.

Dogs had however become a part of the British Army and although they were used during the Second World War as guard dogs and later trained to detect mines, there is no record of Royal Signals using dogs for the delivery of messages during that conflict. Dogs are, of course, now permanently part of the military establishment and are still very much in use at Hong Kong and as guard dogs in other stations.

A dog laying cable.

A Signal Service message carrying dog.

Dogs on exercise at Etaples, circa 1918 – Message carriers were worn at all times.

GHQ Central kennels. Dogs wearing message containers.

Horse drawn pigeon loft.

Chapter 7
The Pigeon Service

The story of the use of pigeons as a message carrying medium in war time is very adequately covered in the book 'Pigeons in Two World Wars', which was published by Colin Osman in 1976, which incorporated 'Pigeons in the Great War' by Lieutenant Colonel A. H. Osman, OBE and 'Pigeons in World War II' by Major W. H. Osman. However as the use of carrier pigeons as a means of conveying messages was practiced by the Royal Engineer Signal Service and later by the Royal Signals it is only appropriate that some details are given in this publication.

Pigeons have been used as message carriers in many previous wars and it is recorded that pigeons relayed the news of Caesar's conquest of Gaul, and in the 13th Century Ghenghis Khan organised a pigeon relay-service across Asia and a large part of Europe. Later the news of Wellington's victory at Waterloo was conveyed by pigeon with the news arriving by this means far in advance of the messenger.

Messages were sent into Paris during the siege of 1870 and 1871. Letters from England were sent from London to Tours where the messages were photographically copied in a much reduced form on thin films of collodian and sent into the capital by carrier pigeon. The film was then relayed onto a screen by magic lantern which was popular at that time. The pigeon service was carried out under extremely adverse conditions during the winter of 1870-1871 but during that time thousands of messages were carried over the Prussian lines and delivered safely to Paris. It is recorded that on 3 February 1871 a single pigeon arrived in Paris carrying 40,000 messages using this early example of the 'micro-film'. In a lecture on this subject Colonel Osman reported that the lecturer, Captain G. G. Aston of the Royal Marine Artillery, gave the following table of figures of the pigeons used (or 'tossed') during the siege of Paris and those that actually arrived (or 'homed') with the message:

". . . MONTH	TOSSED	ARRIVED
September and October 1870	105	22
November	83	17
December	49	12
January, 1871	43	3
February, 1871	22	3
	302	57

". . . "

The percentage of safe arrival was very small, but this was largely due to the fact that this was an emergency service and had been adapted to suit the circumstances. In later conflicts the arrival rate became much higher as birds were trained and were handled by experts.

The British Army used a limited number of pigeons during the Boer War when it became necessary to communicate with the besieged garrison at Ladysmith. Pigeons were used to carry despatches and plans out of Ladysmith and the service proved so successful that a number of small Pigeon Lofts were established by the army.

During the early part of the First World War the use of pigeons was controlled by the Intelligence Corps but in the spring of 1915 pigeons were successfully used to bring back situation reports during the enemy attack on Yprès. As a result of these operations the first Corps Pigeon Service was organised in the Second Corps during the month of May. From this date the growth of the forward Carrier Pigeon Service was rapid. The carrier pigeon had already been recognised as a trustworthy and speedy means of conveying messages over distances which were far greater than the newly-introduced trench wireless set was capable of reaching. Not only were the pigeons quick but they appeared to be untroubled by gun fire whilst in flight and were less susceptible to the effects of gas than human beings.

Pigeon messages went straight from battalion headquarters, or from pigeon posts in the trenches, to Division or Corps Headquarters. As the majority of the messages were intended for the Brigade to which the battalion belonged, some delay was inevitable but it was reduced to a minimum by co-locating the lofts to the nearest signal office of the formation which the bird served. Pigeon messages were treated as Priority and were given preference over all 'less important telephone traffic'. Records show that the message from the trenches could be relied upon to reach the Brigade Headquarters in 10, 15 or 20 minutes according to the distance that the pigeon had to fly. The men in the trenches appreciated the use of pigeons as prior to their introduction quite a number of soldiers had been killed whilst acting as messengers. It was difficult at first to ensure that the soldiers did not over feed the birds and make pets of the carrier pigeons, but this problem was gradually overcome.

As the service increased and more men were trained as 'pigeoneers' (this was prior to the introduction of the trade of Loftsman) a great degree of efficiency was attained, and having trained handlers ensured that the pigeons were properly handled and fed and protected against the rats which infested the trenches.

The new organisation gave a pigeon station at each Brigade sector of the front and at each station was a basket containing four pigeons in charge of a specially trained soldier. In June 1915 the Carrier Pigeon Service was reorganised and an establishment of ten pigeon stations with each army was authorised and a similar number for the Cavalry Corps. In order to cater for this new requirement the enlistment of 60 pigeon 'specialists' was authorised and the service was transferred to the RE Signal Service. The plan of the First Army Pigeon Service for December 1915 shows that 15 Pigeon Stations had been established with 8 reserve 'baskets', giving a total of 202 birds.

As the war progressed it became necessary to increase the service even further and the lessons learned during the Somme offensive showed that there was a need for a mobile 'loft' which could be moved from location to location as the need arose. The proposal for the mobile service called for 6 motor and 60 horse drawn lofts, with the motorised loft holding 50 and horse drawn loft 75 birds, so that

Motor cyclist preparing to deliver pigeons to outstations.

A headquarters pigeon loft.

the new mobile service would give an additional 4,800 pigeons to the Signal Service. The mobile loft proved to be a success as by 1917 it was reported that the service was extremely efficient with several hundred messages being passed by the pigeon service during every battle. The establishment was again increased during July 1917 when the horse drawn lofts were increased to 120 and 6 motor mobile lofts and the use of pigeons had been extended so that they were also used by artillery officers on forward observation duties and by tank crews.

The Pigeon Service at this time had, according to the history of the Royal Engineer Signal Service, far outstripped the forward wireless service in its practical utility but in the later actions of the war, and in particular during a retreat, it was found that the mobile lofts were not as 'mobile' as had been hoped. Horses were difficult to find at short notice and with the roads completely congested during one retreat 40 horse-drawn and motor mobile lofts were lost to the enemy. Most of these had been destroyed by fire and the birds dispersed so that no mobile loft was captured complete with its birds.

The Carrier Pigeon Service continued throughout the war and at the conclusion of the conflict there were 22,000 pigeons in the service, with 150 mobile lofts and 400 pigeoneers.

Following the formation of the Royal Corps of Signals in 1920 the newly formed Corps took over the responsibility for the Pigeon Service and during the years

Delivering pigeons in Italy, circa 1917.

The correct way to hold a pigeon.

Loftsmen loading pigeons into a transit basket, circa 1940.

in between the two wars lofts were established and loftsman became a trade within the Corps.

Training of the birds was, in some cases, combined with other activities and in India one unit carried out a weekly recreational visit to a lake where swimming and a picnic took place. At the same time the pigeons were also taken and despatched back to the unit lines as part of the weekly training programme, thus making it a combination of business with pleasure.

In 1937, with the threat of war becoming increasingly evident, a sub-committee of the Committee of Imperial Defence was set up to consider the use of pigeons in war. The actual outbreak of war in 1939 brought about the expansion of the Carrier Pigeon Service and in 1940, as part of the anti-invasion communication plan, birds were requisitioned from civil lofts and trained to work from military fixed and mobile lofts. Fortunately this service, which was meant to be a back-up communication system if other means failed, was never put to the test.

During the 1939-45 conflict the Royal Signals established 157 Pigeon Lofts, some of which were based in the United Kingdom and others were for use in overseas stations. Of these 130 were 'Fixed' lofts and 27 were 'Mobile' lofts.

Brancepeth Castle, County Durham. A fixed pigeon loft was established in the left tower of the main entrance.

Early in the Second World War, pigeons were carried in bomber aircraft and were released in the event of a crash. A Halifax bomber, which was lost on operations over Germany, on 12 June 1943, presumably near to its target, released its pigeon with a message. The bird 'homed' on 16 June having made a flight of over 400 miles. Likewise the Royal Navy also used pigeons as message carriers. Motor Torpedo Boats operating off the French coast were required to maintain radio silence but were able to relay messages back to base by the use of carrier pigeons. Pigeons were also extensively used by resistance groups working in occupied territories. Such pigeons were delivered to the group by a parachute drop and enabled the group to send messages, or even film, back to England thus obviating the danger of transmitting a message by radio which could be, and often was, intercepted by German radio detector vehicles.

Pigeons were used at Dieppe, D Day and at Arnhem and by both the British and American forces. William of Orange, an Army Pigeon Service bird, was awarded the Animal's VC, the Dickin Medal, for his record flight from Arnhem on 19th September 1945. He was released at 1030 hours and arrived at his loft at 1455 hours the same day, having flown 260 miles, 135 of these miles were

The office and 'young bird' section of the Brancepeth Castle loft.

The abandoned loft was discovered in 1985 and reported to the staff of the Royal Signals Museum. A visit was organised to the castle before renovation work was started on the tower and the loft removed. A photographic record was made by Mr G. Parselle.
The loft had been abandoned in 1945 and the outside door left open so that the loft was used by wild pigeons over the ensuing 40 years.

(above) The 'Service Bird' area.

Remains of the Pigeon Loft unit sign at Brancepeth Castle.

Above: Area ouside the pigeon entrance to the Brancepeth Castle loft.
Below: Pigeons in a military loft in WW2.

William of Orange.
Awarded the Dickin Medal in 1945.

over open sea. William of Orange (Pigeon Number NS 15125) had been bred by Sir William Proctor Smith of Bexton House, Bexton, near Knutsford. He was a mealy cock and was trained by the Army Pigeon Service. At the end of the war Sir William bought William of Orange 'out of service' for £135 and ten years later it was recorded that he was still alive although ''. . .too old to race or breed. . . .' Lady Smith, presented the Dickin Medal, that had been awarded to William of Orange, to the Royal Signals Museum in 1965.

Lofts were established in the Middle East, and in India and Burma where they were manned by the Indian Signal Corps and in these theatres the pigeon distinguished itself in many instances. The publication 'Pigeons in World War II' gives a 'Meritorious Performance List' and it is quite clear that a number of pigeons were killed or lost whilst on active service. A typical entry reads:

'' . . . CC 1418 B.C. Hen.   Was the only one to home from British airborne troops or paratroops in the Normandy operation within 24 hours. The

N.P.S.42 N.S.15125
WILLIAM OF ORANGE
ARMY PIGEON SERVICE
ARNHEM
SEPT. 1944
A F M C 1080
N° 21

The Dicken Medal awarded to William of Orange.

weather was extremely adverse and the birds were detained six days in small containers. Released with message at 08.37 hours on the 7th June, arrived at 06.41 hours on the 8th June (23 hours 4 minutes, including darkness). This pigeon was subsequently lost in a further flight from France. . .''

At the end of the Second World War all Royal Signals pigeon lofts were closed and the trade of Loftsman was removed from the Corps list of tradesmen in 1946.

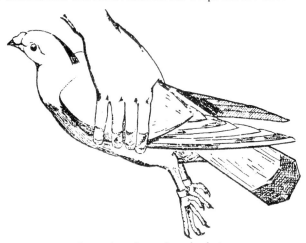

Removing pigeon from basket.

102

Chapter 8
Horses for Courses

As the Royal Corps of Signals was classed as a mounted arm it became inevitable that both officers and men would develop an interest in equestrian sports and in the years following the formation of the Corps, until the outbreak of the Second World War, this interest brought the Corps into the public eye by appearances at the Royal Tournament.

In 1928 the Cavalry Signals at Tidworth organised a motor cycle display based on the popular cavalry musical rides. Meanwhile at Catterick, the Mounted Wing had performed many musical rides at local shows. It was then decided to combine the two displays and have a 'Combined Horse and Motor Cycle Display'. A motor cycle display team was then formed at Catterick Camp, under Lieutenant (later Brigadier) H. R. Firth, and a great deal of training was required, out of normal working hours, before the horses would accept the noise and speed of the motor cycles. By the end of the extensive training one mare would even lie down for the motor cycles to jump over her. Lieutenant (later Brigadier) H. N. Crawford became the manager of the horsed display and in 1933 the Corps introduced the combined display at Olympia. The event was extremely popular with the public, and even the critics (who had been of the opinion that the two types of display would not work) gave an enthusiastic welcome to this new event at the military tournament. Lieutenant (later Brigadier) W. M. Ponsonby and Lieutenant Henry Crawford became two of the finest show jumpers in the Army and won many championships, as did a soldiers' team led by Company Sergeant Major Young. The combined display team had, in 1934, twenty-six horses and during the years 1933 to 1936 the team attended many local engagements ranging from the Woolwich Searchlight Tattoo in the south to the Scottish Command Pageant at Edinburgh in the north and across the Irish Sea to attend the Royal Ulster Agricultural Show at Belfast.

In India the Corps was represented in almost every equestrian event and Captain (later Major General) C. M. F. White won the North of India Tournament. Corps officers also played a full part in the organisation and running the 'Hunts' that had been formed in India. Captain G. S. Hurst, Royal Signals, became Master of the Peshawar Vale Hunt for the years 1932-33 and 1933-34. The Peshawar Vale Hunt had been formed in 1868 and was over the years, a renouned and popular hunt. Captain (later Major General) A. M. W. Whistler became The Master of the Nerbudda Vale Hunt with Sergeant (later Major) R. H. Farlow as the 1st Whip. Many of the soldiers stationed in India became proficient riders who took part in equestrian events that were so much a part of the annual life in India. Units had annual sporting weeks during which time all manner of sport and recreational events were organised. The hunts and unit stables remained a part of the everyday life in India up until the outbreak of war in 1939 and even after that date, although many of the sporting personalities were posted to active units, the younger officers and men who were posted to India were still encouraged to ride during their free time. As late as 1947 weekend and afternoon riding was

Show jumping, 1933. Sergeant Hill on Bertha at Rushmore Arena.

Tandem driving, 1933 at Rushmore Arena.

The Nerbudda Vale Hunt, with the Master, Captain A. M. W. Whistler, and Sergeant R. H. Farlow, 1st Whip.

The Peshawar Vale Hunt.

106

The Peshawar Vale Hunt.

Lieutenant (later Brigadier) H. N. Crawford jumping at one of the many shows
attended by the combined Display Team in 1933.

a popular pastime, although by that time the majority of the unit stables had been
closed. The horses were supplied by locally run stables but the costs were well
within the capability of any young soldier wishing to take part in this type of
recreation.

Meanwhile in the United Kingdom the horse had been replaced in unit
establishments in 1937 and it was only in India that the horse- drawn cable wagon
was still in use. The demise of the horse from the unit establishment was generally
deplored by the officers and men who had spent their life in the Royal Signals
with animals. The interest in equestrian events generally waned once the horse
had been withdrawn although in recent years young officers joining the Royal
Signals have been given basic horsemanship training whilst on their Subalterns
course at the School of Signals at Blandford Camp.

BIBLIOGRAPHY

Adams, Colonel R.M., **Through to 1970, Royal Signals Golden Jubilee,** London 1970.

Cooper, Jilly, **Animals in War,** London 1983.

Hammerton, J.A., **The War Illustrated,** Vol 8, 1918.

Hurst, Captain (Bt Major) G.S., **History of the Peshawar Vale Hunt,** Aldershot 1935.

Nalder, Major General R.F.H., **The Royal Corps of Signals, A History of its antecedents and development,** London 1958.

Osman, Lieutenant Colonel A.H., **Pigeons in the Great War,** London.

Osman, Major W.H., **Pigeons in World War II,** Norwich 1950.

Priestley, R.E., **The Signal Service in the European War of 1914-18 (France),** Chatham 1921.

Wilson, H.W., **With the Flag to Pretoria** (2 Vols), London and **After Pretoria; The Guerilla War,** London 1902.

History of the (Indian) Corps of Signals, New Delhi 1975.

Instructions in Laying and Maintaining Field Telegraph Line, War Office, HMSO 1907.

Instructions on the Use of Carrier Pigeons in War, War Office, HMSO 1917.

Indian Pigeon Service - Manual of Instruction for the use of Homing Pigeons in India and SE Asia, Delhi, 1945.

Manual of Horsemastership, Equitation and Animal Transport, HMSO, London, 1937.

Royal Corps of Signals Combined Horse and Motor Cycle Display, Pictorial Souvenir 1933, Richmond, Yorks 1933.

Royal Signals Display, Pictorial Souvenir, 1934.

The Journal, of the Royal Signals Institution.

The Wire, The Royal Signals Magazine.

INDEX

Air-line Telegraph... 37
Air-line wagon.. 10,29,41,45
Aldershot 11,29,43,55,59
Army Pigeon Service... 97,101
Army Signal School... 75
Army Signal Service.. 34
Arnhem... 97
Arundel.. 32
Ashton, Captain G.G.. 91

Balaclava 1
Belmont... 65
Bengal Sappers and Miners (No 6 Company)...................... 14
Berbera... 61
Beresford, Major C.F.C....................................... 29,31
Bertha (Horse)... 104
Blandford... 10,11
Blandford Camp.. 108
Bloemfontein.. 34
Bohote 61
Bombay Sapper and Miners (A Company)......................... 16
Brancepeth Castle, Co Durham........................ 97,98,99,100
Branding.. 25
Brompton Barracks, Chatham................................... 5
Bullocke, Mr.. 65

Cable cart.............................. 1,2,29,33,36,37,38,39,40
Cable Telegraph Company...................................... 37
Cable wagon.............. 4,5,7,8,11,29,30,37,39,42,46,48,49,52-59,71
Cadwell, Sergeant C.. 34
Camels.. 15,21,25,60-64
Cape Town... 65
Cavalry Staff Corps... 2
Carrier Pigeon Service...................................... 92,94,96
Cobb, Leiutenant F.R... 49
Charging Engine, 550 watt..................................... 80
Colesberg... 31
Collier, Lance Corporal J...................................... 32
Cooke, Sir William... 1
Corps of Signals... 39
Crawford, Lieutenant (Later Brigadier) H.N................... 103,108
C Telegraph Troop, Royal Engineers................... 5,6,10,11,12,49
Cyrus of Persia.. 13

Dakka 15
Danzig 52
De Aar 65
Dera Ismail Khan 75
Dicken Medal 97,101,102
Divisional Telegraph Company 37
Dobrudscha 1
Dogs 85-89
Donaghy, Corporal 78
Dover 2,3,4

Edinburgh 36
Egypt 16,49,50
Electric Telegraph Company 1
Elephants 19,20,21,73,82,83
Enslin 65
Etaples 88
Evelyn Wood Committee 37
Experimental cable cart 29,31,32

Farlow, Sergeant (later Major) R.H 103,106
Field Telegraph Office 1,2,11
Field Telegraph Train 2,3,4
Forge wagon 5
First Army Pigeon Service 92
Firth, Lieutenant (later Brigadier) H.R 103

Genghis Khan 13,91
Godfrey-Faussett, Captain E.G 34

Hamilton, Major A.C 11
Heliograph 13,14
Hill, Sergeant 104
Hong Kong 85
Hurst, Captain G.S 103
Hurst Castle, Hampshire 29
Hythe 29

Indian Signal Corps 70
Intelligence Corps 92

Jalalabad 15,16
Jubbulpore (Jabalpur) 26,28,75

Kadir 82

Karachi... 27,74,75
Kennedy, Captain J.N.C................................ 65
Kimberley... 34,37
Kirkee.. 13
Kitchener, Lieutenant H.H.............................. 11
Kohat... 75

Ladysmith.. 92
Lambert, Captain Montague............................. 5
Limerick Signal Company............................... 44
Loftsman... 92,96,102
Loralai... 75

Mackworth, Lieutentant H. (later Sir Harry)........... 34,61
Madras Sappers and Miners............................. 16
Marco Polo... 13
Marconi Company....................................... 65
Marconi half kilowatt spark set....................... 68
Meerut... 74,75
Mesopotamia... 39,46,47,62
Military Veterinary Hospital, Jubbulpore.............. 26,28
Modder... 65
Mohmand Operations.................................... 22
Mons Barracks, Aldershot.............................. 51
Morse, Samuel... 1
Mount Everest... 71,76

Naini Tal.. 74,75
Nerbudda Vale Hunt.................................... 103,106
Netley... 29
Nobby (Horse number 30091)............................ 50,51

Office wagon... 1,3,5,9

Pack Cable Section..................................... 68
Palestine.. 60
Peshawar... 15,75
Peshawar Field Force.................................. 15
Peshawar Vale Hunt.................................... 103,106,107
Pigeoneer.. 92
Pigeon Loft, horse drawn.............................. 90
Pigeons.. 90—102
Ponsonby, Lieutenant (later Brigadier) W.M............ 103
Pontoon (or Boat) wagon............................... 5,8
Poona.. 13,74,75
Postal Telegraph Companies............................ 12
Post and Telegraphs Department of India............... 19

Quetta, India 23, 74, 75

Raglan, Lord 1
Rawalpindi, India 74,75
Razmak, India 68
Razmak Brigade Signal Section 68
Razmak Moveable Column 65
Richardson, Lieutenant Colonel E.H. 85
Risalpur, India 74,75
Roberts, Lord 34
Rorkee, India 13
Rowlands Castle, Hampshire 41
Royal Engineers Signal Service 39, 65, 85, 91, 92, 94
Royal Corps of Signals (title) 39, 94
Royal Engineers School, Chatham 2, 6
Royal Ulster Agricultural Show 103

Savage, Lieutenant G.R.R. 13
Scottish Command Pageant 103
School of Signals 108
Secunderabad, India 75
Selby, Lieutenant H.C. 13
Shoeburyness 85
Sialkot, India 69,74,75
Signal Training School 75
Smijth-Windham, Lieutenant (later Brigadier) W.R. 71
Smith, Sir William Proctor 101
Somaliland Field Force 61
Somme 92
South Arabia 63,64
Stopford, Lieutenant George Montague 1
Store wagon 5

Telegraph Battalion RE 12,29,31,35,36
Thompson, Lieutenant E.C. 71
Tidworth, Hampshire 103
Trimulgherry, India 74

Units — British Army
1st Division, Telegraph Battalion RE 12,29,36,61
2nd Division, Telegraph Battalion RE 12
1st Divisional Signals 50,51
2nd Divisional Signals 58
City of London Signals 56
56th (London) Divisional Signals 55
Signal Training Centre, Maresfield 55

Indian Army
A Corps Signals (India)................................... 27,71,74
B Corps Signals (India)....................................... 71,74
1st Indian Divisional Signals.................................... 74
2nd Indian Divisional Signals................................... 74
3rd Indian Divisional Signals................................... 74
4th Indian Divisional Signals................................... 74
1st Cavalry Brigade Signal Troop............................... 74
2nd Cavalry Brigade Signal Troop............................ 69,74
3rd Cavalry Brigade Signal Troop............................... 75
4th Cavalry Brigade Signal Troop............................... 75
Kohat District Signals... 75
Signal Training Battalion, Jubbulpore........................... 28
Signal Training Centre, Jubbulpore............................. 75
Waziristan District Signals..................................... 75
Wireless Section.. 68
W/T Experimental Section..................................... 75
Wireless Telegraph Companies.................................. 37
Zhob Signal Section... 75

Varna 1

Wana Column... 77
Waterloo.. 91
Wheatstone, Professor Sir Charles............................... 1
Whistler, Captain (later Major General) A.M.W............... 103,106
White, Captain (later Major General) C.M.F.................... 103
William of Orange.. 97,101,102
Wireless Set Type C....................................... 65,68,77,81
Wireless Set No 1.......................... 69,70,72,73,78,79,82,83,
Wireless Set No 22.. 84
Wire wagon (see cable wagon)
Wireless wagons.. 65,66,67
Wolseley, Major General Sir Garnet J.......................... 62
Woolwich Searchlight Tattoo.................................. 103

Yak.. 70,73,76
Yakdan.. 27,70,71
Young, CSM... 103